Living the Days of Lent 2012

Edited by Ellen Dauwer, SC, and Mary McCormick, SC

Paulist Press
New York / Mahwah, NJ

Copyright © 2012 by Paulist Press, Inc.

ISBN 978-0-8091-4711-3

Published by Paulist Press
997 Macarthur Boulevard
Mahwah, New Jersey 07430

www.paulistpress.com

Printed and bound in the
United States of America

Introduction

Each year the Church gifts us with forty days of Lent, followed by fifty days of Easter. During this quarter of the Church year we have the opportunity to enter into the Paschal Mystery as fully as possible. Our everyday lives are filled with times of suffering and dying as well as times of rising and renewing. In Lent we are invited to unite our individual times of suffering and death with those of the broader Church and ultimately with those of Jesus.

The pages that follow were written by Sisters of Charity of New York and Sisters of Charity of Saint Elizabeth of New Jersey. As daughters of Elizabeth Ann Seton, they minister to those who suffer in many ways: in hospitals and hospices, in classrooms and clinics, and in parishes and pastoral centers.

May our Lenten journey this year be one that will enable us to touch our pain, the pain of others, and the pain of the world in a way that will open us all to the healing touch of Jesus.

Contributors
(in alphabetical order)

Sister Regina Bechtle, SC
Sister Sheila Brosnan, SC
Sister Mary Canavan, SC
Sister Anita Constance, SC
Sister Maureen Corcoran, SC
Sister Mary Ann Daly, SC
Sister Ellen Dauwer, SC
Sister Margaret Donegan, SC
Sister Kathleen Flanagan, SC
Sister Cheryl France, SC
Sister Barbara Garland, SC
Sister Vivienne Joyce, SC
Sister Eileen T. Kelly, SC
Sister Mary E. Mc Cormick, SC
Sister Noreen Neary, SC
Sister Ellen Rose O' Connell, SC

From Ashes to Joy

*"But when you fast, put oil on your head and
wash your face....your Father who sees
in secret will reward you."*
—Matthew 6:17–18

For centuries, wearing ashes—a sign of public humiliation—acknowledges Christian penitents as sinners, those
who have turned away from God. During the ritual we are
reminded that we come from the earth and at the end of
our lives we shall return to the earth.

But viewed in the context of Easter, Ash Wednesday
should be a day of great joy. As the *Exultet* proclaims, "O
happy fault!" Only by acknowledging our sinful nature and
repenting for the falsities and excesses of our lives can we
change. Only by turning toward God can we be assured
that we are more than dust, that we have been ransomed,
that far more awaits us than the grave.

**Today, as I wear the ashes of humiliation, may I be joyful,
for today is the acceptable time to turn to God, to accept
the grace of God. Today is the day of salvation!**

Readings: Joel 2:12–18; Psalm 51:3–6, 12–14, 17;
2 Corinthians 5:20—6:2; Matthew 6:1–6,16–18

The Daily Cross

*Then he said to them all, "If any want to become
my followers, let them deny themselves and take up
their cross daily and follow me. For those who want
to save their life will lose it, and those who
lose their life for my sake will save it."*
—Luke 9:23–24

In response to Peter's declaration that Jesus is the Messiah
of God, Jesus teaches his followers what being the
Messiah, the anointed one, really means. He breaks apart
the traditional meaning: the king of Davidic lineage who
will deliver Israel and restore its golden age in the worldly
sense. Jesus teaches us that self-denial and suffering even
to the point of death lead to freedom and everlasting life.
By reversing the curse of the first man's disobedience, the
Son of Man's obedience even unto death ransoms us as
daughters and sons of God.

**Today, as I reflect on the paradoxes of the Gospel message,
may I joyfully accept the crosses in my life, viewing those
burdens as my participation in God's salvation of the world.**

Readings: Deuteronomy 30:15–20;
Psalm 1:1–4, 6; Luke 9:22–25

Presence

"The wedding guests cannot mourn as long as the bridegroom is with them, can they?"
—Matthew 9:15

Happy are those who know this! So many days are filled with so many details and so little time to search what lies beneath. Activity can eclipse reality, and I can forget that Jesus is with me in the midst of it all. In the messiness of my days, some boring, some hectic, some painful, some joyful, is the Bridegroom present? In this particular moment that puzzles, amuses, frightens, or challenges me, where are you, Jesus? Are you the reality in the depth of my action, in the core of my being? There is no mourning when I recognize your abiding presence!

Let me take the time to name you in the particulars of this day. Call me to look for you in its joys, challenges, surprises, and ordinariness. Let me not close my eyes in sleep tonight before I have celebrated your faithfulness to me.

Readings: Isaiah 58:1–9; Psalm 51:3–6, 18–19; Matthew 9:14–15

Fidelity for the Long Haul

And he got up, left everything, and followed him.
—Luke 5:28

How easy it would be if the "follow me" (Luke 5:27) was a once-only request. Leaving everything behind and starting over once doesn't sound like a bad deal. It is the daily following, the long-term fidelity, that requires me to examine the cost of discipleship. The everyday conversions that are necessary to prevent me from falling into the trap of feeling righteous have their cost. Am I willing to cast my lot with the other sinners, the outcasts? Can I be a follower of Jesus if I don't?

Who are the "sinners" that I shun? Are they of a different economic class, political party, religion, or nationality? Do I ever catch myself in the role of the Pharisee?

Today, I will judge only myself. Today, I will recall that Jesus' mercy is with each and every sinner in this world, including me. Today, I will view reality from the place of the excluded and repent for what I have failed to see from my place of righteousness.

Readings: Isaiah 58:9–14;
Psalm 86:1–6, 18–19; Luke 5:27–32

First Sunday of Lent, *February 26*

Impelled by the Spirit

*The Spirit immediately drove him out into
the wilderness....and he was with the
wild beasts; and the angels waited on him.
—Mark 1:12–13*

The rainbow promise and the dove came to Noah
after his forty days with a boatload of rescued beasts.
Like a dove the Spirit descended on Jesus
as he came up out of Jordan's waters,
and he heard, "You are my Son, the Beloved."
"...the Spirit immediately drove him out into the
    wilderness....
forty days, tempted by Satan...with the wild beasts."

The rainbow covenant with the whole earth promises
that the wild beasts, wild times, and wild places
are all part of our good space and place as the
    beloved of God.
A profound realization of whose we are,
a personal epiphany of how beloved we are;
do you remember such?

We may then be startled by the immediacy
of "being driven" by the Spirit
to our own "wilderness" of fears and temptations.
And then we remember: angels waited on him.

**Make me know your ways, O LORD...
for you I wait all day long. (Psalm 25:4, 5)**

Readings: Genesis 9:8–15; Psalm 25: 4–9; 1 Peter 3:18–22;
Mark 1:12–15

For the Least among Us

"Just as you did it to one of the least of these who are members of my family, you did it to me."
—Matthew 25:40

Do you know where your local food cupboard is? Have you ever visited your parish "Worn Again" shop? Do you support your homeless shelter and soup kitchen, the community hospital or local prison?

There is no end to the opportunities to help others in need today—locally, nationally, and globally. As the gap between the haves and the have-nots widens and the numbers who live below the poverty line increase, the challenge to us increases dramatically as well.

"If you wish to be perfect, go, sell your possessions, and give the money to the poor;...then come, follow me" (Matthew 19:21). These words are now addressed to us. Will we too let our earthly possessions come between Jesus and us?

Can we give away a favorite possession today to a person in need of it?

Readings: Leviticus 19:1–2, 11–18; Psalm 19:8–10, 15; Matthew 25:31–46

The Prayer of Jesus

"But whenever you pray, go into your room and shut the door and pray to your Father who is in secret; and your Father who sees in secret will reward you."
—Matthew 6:6

Jesus taught his followers to pray by word and example. He taught them the basics of prayer in the Our Father. Another time, he showed the importance of prayer when he spent the whole night in prayer. He urged them to pray in secret, and at other times provided an opportunity for shared prayer. He prayed to heal, to cast out our demons, to forgive sins, and for courage to undergo his suffering and death. When did he not pray?

Karl Rahner, SJ, in his book *Encounters with Silence*, tells us that he feels his prayer is like calling down a deep well. He hears back only the sound of his own voice. Or, he asks, is it that my whole life is my prayer and eternity is God's answer?

**Lord, teach me to pray and to trust
that you do hear and will respond.**

Readings: Isaiah 55:10–11; Psalm 34:4–7, 16–17, 18–19; Matthew 6:7–15

Power to Believe

"This generation...asks for a sign."
—Luke 11:29

Much wants more. Jesus had shown by many signs and wonders that he was the Son of Man (whom we know to be the Son of God). But these were not enough. Some still did not believe. Some even said he received his power from the devil. It seemed not to matter whose power was at work as long as some extraordinary event broke into the dullness of the day. Many people followed Jesus to be astounded, entertained.

And I, Lord, do I too feel dry and in doubt if you do not extend extraordinary graces to keep me believing and trusting in you? Must my life be one of seeking spiritual consolations? Does my faith depend upon having some modern-day Jonah capture the headlines? Is the miracle of grace given over and over to me not sufficient for me to live a holy life?

"Lord, I do believe, help Thou my unbelief." Let us recite this prayer often today to strengthen our faith.

Readings: Jonah 3:1–10;
Psalm 51:3–4, 12–13, 18–19;
Luke 11:29–32

An Open Door

"Ask...search...knock...." The migrants,
the homeless, the desperate, the fearful,
the needy relentlessly seek love and mercy and
relief from our benevolent God.
—Matthew 7:7

I long to be part of that great multitude that trusts
unwaveringly in the largesse of our Creator and the
promise that God is my Advocate.

The lavish, unmerited love of God stirs the depths of
my soul. My spirit urges me to seek new vistas of
unity and healing. Gifts received are gifts to be
given.

From the beginning of life to the end, and at every
moment in between, I am cherished and protected
by God, my loving Father and Mother.

Blessed be God, and the parents who respond to the
needs of their children with tender faithfulness.

My heart is exuberant in praise of God's effusive and
generative love. May it enable me to treat others
the way that I would like to be treated.

**During the lengthening days of Lent, the door to oneness
with Christ opens wide. "Ask...search...knock."**

Readings: Esther C:12, 14–16, 23–25; Psalm 138:1–3, 7–8;
Matthew 7:7–12

Readiness for Worship

"When you are offering your gift at the altar, if you remember that your brother or sister has something against you, leave your gift there before the altar and go; first be reconciled to your brother or sister, and then come and offer your gift."
—Matthew 5:23–24

Anger has many faces: fury, annoyance, displeasure, and even stony impassivity. Worship must be postponed for reconciliation!

O God, anger is a powerful and complex gift that is part of the fabric of my being. You know how easy it is to be caught in the riptide of anger and resentment with people who are most familiar to me. Sustain me in patience and kindliness when someone resists my efforts to be reconciled.

Let your spirit of love embrace me as I struggle to dispel the cords of anger in my contentious relationships. Help me to change the face of the earth.

It is time to come to the table. Jesus is longing to be one with us in Eucharist.

Readings: Ezekiel 18:21–28; Psalm 130:1–4, 5–8; Matthew 5:20–26

A Message from the Mountaintop

*"He makes his sun rise on the evil and on the good,
and sends rain on the righteous and
on the unrighteous."*
—Matthew 5:45

Day in and day out, the warm, light mantle of God's love covers both the deserving and the undeserving. Perfection, holiness, means joining our God to bless all at dawn and bless all at end of day. It means that in rhythm with the heartbeat of our God, I pray for those who disagree with me, who oppose me, or who are choosing sinful paths.

I meet the enemy every day, sometimes from within and sometimes in my surroundings.

O God, reveal to me the love of the Father. It is a great leap of faith for me to love with great magnitude. If such love proves too difficult for me, I am counting on you to act on my behalf. I know that your love is unwearied and benevolent in all times.

God's love is steadfast and everlasting! (Psalm 118:29)

Readings: Deuteronomy 26:16–19; Psalm 119:1–2, 4–5, 7–8; Matthew 5:43–48

Second Sunday of Lent, *March 4*

Transfiguration

*Jesus...led them up a
high mountain apart, by themselves.*
—Mark 9:2

Take me apart.
Literally.
Take me apart.
Plan by plan,
Terror by terror,
Question by question.
Or, at least when I fall apart,
Let it be into your dazzlingly beloved arms.
May my inner self, so exposed to your countenance,
emerge as a mirror of your transfigured glory.

Today, I will take some time apart to hear and see only you.

Readings: Genesis 22:1–2, 9–13, 15–18;
Psalm 116:10, 15–17, 18–19;
Romans 8:31–34; Mark 9:2–10

Forgive and REMEMBER

"Forgive, and you will be forgiven...."
—Luke 6:37

Our world is full of "forgiving" problems. Wars begin and never end, often in the name of religion. Then there are the smaller "wars" within families, among friends, within ourselves. It seems so hard to find a way to reconciliation, to say simply, "I'm sorry. Forgive me."

If I am honest, forgiving is never easy. There is something inside me that feels a loss when I forgive. Sometimes forgiveness doesn't seem to remove the deep hurt, the guilt that can consume.

I once read that the challenge is not to *forgive and forget*, but to *forgive and remember*. As I try to forgive myself while I remember my weaknesses, I am touched deeply in soul and heart. In this way, and uniting with the cross of redemption, I also touch deeply into God's love.

As Luke continues, "Give [forgive] and there will be gifts for you...shaken together, running over..." (Luke 6:38).

Readings: Daniel 9:4–10; Psalm 79:8, 9, 11, 13; Luke 6:36–38

In Word and in Deed

"They do not practice what they [preach]....
They do all their deeds to be seen by others...."
—Matthew 23:3, 5

"Action on behalf of justice and participation in the transformation of the world appear to us as a constitutive dimension of the preaching of the Gospel...of the Church's mission for the redemption of the human race" (*Justice in the World*, 1971).

This is what Matthew is trying to say to us. We are all preachers of the Gospel. Called to participate in the transformation of the world, we are challenged to look at the places we influence, the people we see (and do not see) and perhaps reject due to differences.

Ask: How am I participating in the mission of the Gospel and preaching it day by day? Are the works I do inappropriate or incomplete because they please the powerful and not the humble?

Tough questions, aren't they, but we are challenged to preach the Gospel and practice a transforming justice.

Readings: Isaiah 1:10, 16–20;
Psalm 50:8–9, 16–17, 21, 23;
Matthew 23:1–12

The Cup of Blessing

*"Are you able to drink the cup that
I am about to drink?"*
—Matthew 20:22

Why are some cups filled with hardship and others not? What is in the mind of God as he asks each of us to accept a particular hurt or illness or limitation? These are the *cups* that Jesus holds out to us at different times in our lives. Are we able to drink these cups with Jesus?

What do you think God asks of you in this moment of time? What is your cup, flowing over into a life of grace and mercy? Will you answer, as the apostles did, "We are able"?

**Pray slowly with Ignatius Loyola: *Take, Lord, and receive
all my liberty, my memory, my understanding, and my entire will.
All I have and call my own, you have given to me; to you,
Lord, I return it. Everything is yours; do with it what you will.
Give me only your love and your grace. That is enough
for me (Spiritual Exercises, 234).***

Readings: Jeremiah 18:18–20; Psalm 31:5–6, 14–16;
Matthew 20:17–28

Meeting God

*The rich man said, "...if someone goes to them
from the dead, they will repent."*
—Luke 16:31

God of creation, each day from the rising of the sun to its setting, you touch us with your presence. How could the rich man have missed you? Did he not know you in the splendor of the cosmos, in the stars of the heavens and the quiet constancy of the sun, in the strength of the mountains, and the tranquility of the lakes? Did he not meet you in the animals that roam the earth and in the encouraging word and helpful hand of a colleague? Did he not see you in the poor man lying at his gate, longing for food?

Loving God, you so want to be a part of our lives. Always, you invite us to share your life. Open our hearts that we might recognize you in our surroundings and rejoice in your presence. We praise you, O God. There is no God like you.

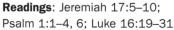

Today, let us be aware of the many signs of God's presence.

Readings: Jeremiah 17:5–10;
Psalm 1:1–4, 6; Luke 16:19–31

All Good Gifts

"He sent his son to them....But when the tenants saw the son, they said to themselves, 'This is the heir; come, let us kill him and get his inheritance.'"
—Matthew 21:37–38

Bountiful God, you give many gifts to us your people whom you love. You scatter your goodness with abandon and you shower your kindness upon all creation. However, we quickly forget that you are the giver of all the gifts we have received. How possessive we become of what you have given so freely. How easily we take ownership. When your Son comes seeking the fruits of your gifts, we are threatened. We fear he will claim our possessions and so we resent him and kill him.

Grant, O God, that we might remember that all we have comes from your generosity. Let us receive your gifts with open hands and share them so they will bring to the world the peace you want.

Let us reflect on God's gifts. How can we share them today to reveal God's presence?

Readings: Genesis 37:3–4, 12–13, 17–28; Psalm 105:16–21; Matthew 21:33–43, 45–46

Saturday, *March 10*

Compassion

"But while he was still far off, his father saw him and
was filled with compassion; he ran and put
his arms around him and kissed him."
—Luke 15:20–21

What an incredible experience! I could hardly believe my eyes. As I dragged my way home, aware of my foolishness, knowing my sin, ready to beg forgiveness, O Compassionate One, there you were, peering down the road, waiting, longing for my return. From a distance, you knew me and you ran to embrace me. I fell into your arms. I rested my head on your heart. Once again, I was with you. It was time to celebrate.

O forgiving God, how can I ever fathom your compassion! When I stand before you and let your loving eyes gaze upon me, I feel peace and I sense your joy.

With simplicity and humility, let us come before our God that we might know the warmth of his loving embrace.

Readings: Micah 7:14–15, 18–20;
Psalm 103:1–4, 9–12; Luke 15:1–3, 11–32

Holy Zeal

"Zeal for your house will consume me."
—John 2:17; cf. Psalm 69:9

Money changers and temple-offering providers did
    service
in the Passover necessities for regular worshipers.
Religious observances are down-to-earth matters.
The wisdom of our times would tell Jesus
he needed to work on anger management.
A whip of cords, overturned tables, spilled coins,
released birds and beasts, these signs shake
workers and onlookers into protests.
How dare you do this? What sign do you offer to
    justify such ranting and raging?
*Zeal for the holiness of his Father's house consumes
    him!*
Do we ever see pleading for justice, a raging for
    mercy, a forceful voice of opposition
as anger, as "madness"? Do we dismiss genuine
    passion as "emotional hype"?
Do we hear the mighty pounding of the Heart of the
    Holy One
who sees and hears us trivialize the sign working in
    the depths of the Passionate One?
They heard Jesus "threaten" the temple; it was they
    who would destroy the Temple he is.

Your law, O Lord, is perfect. Revive my soul! (Psalm 19:7)

Readings: Exodus 20:1–17; Psalm 19:8, 9, 10, 11;
1 Corinthians 1:22–25; John 2:13–25

Healing

When shall I come and behold the face of God?
—Psalm 42:2

There are times when we find ourselves in situations where we'd rather not be, physically, emotionally, spiritually. We want to be made whole but we want wholeness on *our* terms. We bargain, negotiate, make deals with God to be free of distress and achieve the well-being that will bring us joy. The call is to trust and accept God's ways to be in harmony with ourselves.

Sometimes we may find God's ways too difficult or troublesome. Just as Naaman was disappointed and angry about how God chose to bring healing to him, we too want God to do it our way. We forget that healing and wholeness often come through the intervention of others.

Let us pray for the grace to be a loving agent for God in our world today and rejoice when God's grace and healing are present to us in another.

Readings: 2 Kings 5:1–15;
Psalm 42:2, 3; 43:3, 4; Luke 4:24–30

The Joy of Forgiveness

Peter asked Jesus, "Lord, if my brother sins against me, how often must I forgive him?" ...Jesus answered, "Not seven times, but seventy–seven times."
—cf. Matthew 18:21

Pardon and forgiveness are gifts that express God's great love for us. No matter that we have failed to act as disciples of Jesus, we still encounter the tender and loving God who never seeks retribution nor desires retaliation.

Grace urges us to be people who are ready and open to move from the dark crevices in our lives to the brilliant light that holds and speaks the truth. God's ways will resonate within us, find a home there. They will allow us to be receptive to the mercy that reaches far beyond ourselves.

In that place we come to know that our lives are meant, not to be held tightly, but rather open to the merciful forgiveness God offers. We, in turn, need to share this gift of forgiveness with others. In so doing, we are living as God's children, sisters and brothers of Jesus.

"...forgive us our debts as we also have forgiven our debtors" (Matthew 6:12).

Readings: Daniel 3:25, 34–43; Psalm 25:4–9; Matthew 18:21–35

Attentive Discipleship

*[Moses said]... "For what other great nation
has a god so near to it as the LORD our God
is whenever we call to him? "*
—Deuteronony 4:6

God is calling us today to *attentive discipleship*!

Our purpose in life is rooted in "who we are" and "what we do" but more significantly in "whose we are": people created in the likeness of the divine, bearing the very DNA of God within...how awesome!

Therefore, we are challenged to be faithful to our personal development and spiritual growth, always looking beyond ourselves for the sake of others, for the sake of the reign of God, the mission of Jesus.

We are called to be a SIGN of what God has done for us. We are entrusted with the Gospel of Jesus to live our faith with joy. In doing so, others may see our blessings and be drawn to life with God in Christ.

In gratitude as we live our commitment each day, may we proclaim The Story with conviction!

Readings: Deuteronomy 4:1, 5–9;
Psalm 147:12–13, 15–16, 19–20;
Matthew 5:17–19

The Cost of Discipleship

"Whoever is not with me is against me, and whoever does not gather with me scatters."
—Luke 11:23

Was there ever a clearer directive from Jesus about his expectations for his followers? If you want to follow me, listen to my voice. Then do what I say. Do what I do.

Doing as Jesus did is a learned art. It takes belief in him, trust in his word and reflection, not only on the words and actions of Jesus, but on my life. Where am I called to respond as Jesus did in this present time of my life? What would Jesus do in this conflict? In this moment of forgiveness? In this moment of decision?

Being a disciple of Jesus demands courage and commitment but also reflection. Choose one current event or issue presently in my life. What does Jesus ask of me? How can I bring Jesus to this moment?

Readings: Jeremiah 7:23–28; Psalm 95:1–2, 6–9; Luke 11:14–23

God's Reign Is Near, Is Now

*Jesus [replied], "You shall love your
neighbor as yourself."*
—Mark 12:28

We live in a topsy-turvy world. Racial hatreds still abound. Sacred scriptures are burned in the name of religion. Drugs rule countries, cause wars, and wreck countless lives. Famines, floods, and earthquakes cause endless suffering. Yet today's Gospel proclaims that we are not far from God's reign.

How does this happen? My intention to love makes all the difference—not a love that is merely a spoken word, but love that consumes the heart, the mind, and the soul. It is a love that remembers to stop to look at the gifts of the world around us and praises the God who created them: the sunset that causes us surprise, the miracle of the seasons bringing change, the joy of new life in buds and rebirth.

I see God's reign in the lives of people touched by disasters, in the generosity of response to people in need, in care and concern for the sick and dying.

**How can I bring God's reign by loving my
God in neighbors and in myself?**

Readings: Hosea 14:2–10;
Psalm 81:6–11, 14, 17; Mark 12:28–34

Differences

For I desire steadfast love and not sacrifice....
—Hosea 6:6

Once again Jesus hits the mark with his insight into human nature. How easy it is for me to look with a feeling of superiority as I reflect on the foibles of others. It may not be the "tax collectors" that Jesus speaks of in today's Gospel, but it could well be the "political other" that I disdain: the liberal, the conservative, the immigrant. Whatever the title, Jesus calls me to pay attention to my own shortcomings, to own my sin, to be loving and accepting of differences.

My dentist likes to listen to radio talk shows. As a captive in the dentist chair, I've had to endure many opinions different from my own. Have I changed my outlook? Not really, but I have learned there are many good people who think differently. Should I call this a blessing, or perhaps God's sense of humor?

Pick out someone who differs from you in your views.
Spend the day remembering them in a loving way.

Readings: Hosea 6:1–6; Psalm 51:3–4, 18–21; Luke 18:9–14

Fourth Sunday of Lent, *March 18*

Saved by Love

"...that the world might be saved through him."
—John 3:17

In my world of clutter, busyness, and excess, saving and letting go can be a preoccupation, not just of possessions, but of commitments, relationships, and even ideas.

You have saved me, God, through Jesus your Son, because you love me. Dare I use love rather than convenience, preference, or habit as the criterion for my safekeeping or relinquishing?

**Today, with my heart set on Jesus, I will make
love the standard for my choices.**

Readings: 2 Chronicles 36:14–16, 19–23; Psalm 137:1–6;
Ephesians 2:4–10; John 3:14–21

Monday, *March 19*,
Solemnity of Saint Joseph

Heeding Instructions

*An angel of the Lord appeared
to him in a dream....*
—Matthew 1:20

It may take an angel in a dream for me to stretch the boundaries beyond which I have feared venturing before. So, too, for St. Joseph, whose commitment to the will of God made him instrumental in the unfolding of salvation history.

Is there an angel beckoning me forward from a well-intentioned resolution based on old assumptions? Is there a dream instructing me night after night, only to dissolve with the dawn, unheeded?

Tonight, I will open my inner eyes to the appearance of angels and ready my soul for the wisdom in my dreams. Tomorrow's fidelity to God's plan requires it.

Readings: 2 Samuel 7:4–5, 12–14, 16; Psalm 89:2–5, 27, 29; Romans 4:13, 16–18, 22; Matthew 1:16, 18–21, 24

Healing and Wholeness

*When Jesus saw him lying there and knew that he had
been there a long time, he said to him,
"Do you want to be made well?"*
—John 5:6

In today's Gospel, Jesus meets an infirm man one Sabbath day and offers him healing: "Stand up, take your mat and walk" (John 5:8). The man does so, and is healed.

But there's more to the story. When Jesus meets the man later on, he urges him to abandon his sinful ways, lest something worse befall him. Was his physical infirmity somehow connected with sinful behavior, and was he ashamed that Jesus was aware of his sins? We can only guess. But after this second encounter, he reports Jesus to the Jewish authorities. Curing on the Sabbath was another accusation against Jesus, one ultimately leading to his arrest and crucifixion.

Let us search our hearts and acknowledge our own sinfulness and need of healing. Let us pray this day for the healing of others who are afflicted in body, mind, or spirit.

Readings: Ezekiel 47:1–9, 12;
Psalm 46:2–3, 5–6, 8–9; John 5:1–16

The God of Jesus

The LORD *is near to all who call on him,*
to all who call on him in truth.
—Psalm 145:18

Jesus' identification with God as *his* Father was a source of great scandal to the authorities. Yahweh, the One God, was to be treated with the utmost reverence. Even to utter his name was somehow to demean his reality. But Jesus both identified himself with God and performed marvelous deeds usually ascribed only to God. The religious leaders felt they had to stop such blasphemy. They were blind to the possibility that Yahweh was beyond their understanding. Their solution: destroy the one who challenged their definition of God.

Perhaps this is a time to learn more about our own faith, using insights of modern theology to deepen and challenge some of our earlier understanding. And it could be a time to learn more about the mystery of faith as understood by other traditions.

Lent is a time to attend to our faith in all of its dimensions.
Pray for new insights into the wonder and mystery of God,
whose reality can never be exhausted.

Readings: Isaiah 49:8–15; Psalm 145:8–9, 13–14, 17–18;
John 5:17–30

Glory

*"How can you believe when you accept glory
from one another and do not seek the glory that
comes from the one who alone is God?"*
—John 5:44

Glory—the presence of God made manifest. Jesus never tires of inviting us to the new life we experience when our hearts are open to God. Today will bring unanticipated gifts and blessings. He also warns us: watch out for spiritual materialism by which we think our value is dependent on our efforts or the approval of religious elite. Allow eternal life to leap from the pages of Scripture into the NOW of everyday life. Receive this day as a gift from God who looks on us with love.

Let us allow our hearts to be moved by the witness of Jesus who sought out the weak, the poor, the lonely, and those shunned. Beware of the status quo of all forms of exclusion. May we be true to our deepest selves. Love the ones no one loves.

**Practice kindness that our works may testify to
the risen humanity of Jesus.**

Readings: Exodus 32:7–14;
Psalm 106:19–23; John 5:31–47

Turning Points

"You know me, and you know where I am from."
—John 7:28

The Feast of the Tabernacles celebrates God's presence to the Jewish people when existence was precarious: in exile in the desert. Jesus goes to Jerusalem without telling his disciples. He places himself in the midst of the people, knowing there are many questions, much confusion, and even threatening hostility. We enter the story in light of the Paschal Mystery, and we know how real the threat is. He shares his self-understanding: Jesus is sent by God. We cannot help but anticipate the suffering to come. This is a turning point in the life of Jesus coming to be with us to suffer with us. Jesus still comes from the heart of God to be near the brokenhearted and save those who are crushed in spirit.

Are you facing your own turning point? Have you spoken your truth? Are you opening your heart in prayer or loving action to your neighbor? Will you reach out to someone who is brokenhearted or crushed in spirit?

Readings: Wisdom 2:1, 12–22; Psalm 34:17–21, 23; John 7:1–2, 10, 25–30

Expectations

*"Surely the Messiah does not come
from Galilee, does he?"*
—John 7:41

Think about it—what irony! The hearers are reminded of a learned religious view of reality that taught them not to expect the Christ to come from Galilee. Sincere religious understanding was closing minds and hearts. Today, hearing these words, the irony runs through us: according to what we believe, Galilee is *exactly* where Jesus the Christ comes from! Nicodemus reminds them *and us* of the inner law of Love: give "the other" a hearing and see how "the other" lives. Often we are not open to what we do not expect. Now, as then, we must be careful to keep our hearts open to recognize the truth in unexpected people and places, the truth of God's compassion and love for us.

Lord, teach me to have an open mind and heart.

Readings: Jeremiah 11:18–20;
Psalm 7:2–3, 9–12; John 7:40–53

Fifth Sunday of Lent, *March 25*

The Coming of the Hour

"It is for this reason that I have come to this hour."
—John 12:27

Festivities abound, Gentiles come
seeking Jesus, asking his obvious friend; friends going
   to tell him.
Strange answer: "The hour has come for the Son of
   Man to be glorified."
The somber tone: wheat grains dying for a rich harvest;
loving life and losing it; serving by following; the
   Father honoring...

Conflicted, afflicted by the coming of "this hour," Jesus
   admits he is deeply "troubled"
yet knows his reason for being, this here/now.
Again he says, "Father,"
not "save me from this hour" but "glorify your name."
Thunderous to some, or angelic, the voice declares,
   "I have...and I will again."
Jesus plainly says, "This voice...for your sake not mine."

Have I felt inner rumbling, ominous impending?
Mixed anticipation and fear of the coming, incoming,
   unknown?
Have I glibly named the troubling in Jesus a
   foreknowing of his days ahead?
Is there in him a thunderous welcoming the *sign* of
   Gentiles' coming?

Holy Indwelling, let me know your voice.
Sustain in me a willing spirit!

Readings: Jeremiah 31:31–34; Psalm 51:3–4, 12–15;
Hebrews 5:7–9; John 12:20–33

Monday, *March 26*, Solemnity of the
Annunciation of the Lord

Overshadowed

*Here I am, Lord....I delight to do
your will, O my God...*
—Psalm 40: 8a, 9a

Your call weaves in and
out of my childhood,
Till on the edge of adulthood
you overshadowed me.

Since then, call and response
have taken many forms,
Till one winter afternoon
you came in overshadow again.

Somehow it seemed
that yes was enough,
But your call persists
and pulls at me.

Speak, Lord, your
servant is listening.

Help me to listen to you, Lord, that I may discern your will.

Readings: Isaiah 7:10–14, 8:10;
Psalm 40:7–8, 8–9, 10, 11;
Hebrews 10:4–10; Luke 1:26–38

Listening and Understanding

"The one who sent me is true, and I declare to the world what I have heard from him."
—John 8:26

Have you ever been engaged in a conversation and felt as if you were speaking another language with the other person? In today's Gospel Jesus must have felt as if he were speaking another language to the people. Their literal interpretation of his message must have frustrated him. Yet some understood, for we read: "As he was saying these things, many believed in him" (John 8:30).

How do I listen to the words of Jesus in Scripture and in my life? How do I listen to other people? Do I listen with the ears of faith and hear the meaning *under* the words? Or do I listen only on the surface?

Today I will make an extra attempt to listen to Jesus in my heart, in Scripture, and in others: to hear under their words and to understand their meaning.

Readings: Numbers 21:4–9; Psalm 102:2–3,16–18,19–21; John 8:21–30

Free to Be Ourselves

*"You will know the truth, and the
truth will make you free."*
—John 8:32

How do we know if we are free? The Jews in today's Gospel thought they were free because they were not enslaved. They assumed that freedom was the opposite of slavery, but Jesus was speaking of a deeper freedom: freedom from sin and freedom for love.

When we are truly free, we are truly ourselves. We see with our own eyes, we hear with our own ears, and we speak with our own lips. We love without condition and we free others to be themselves. This is the freedom Jesus was speaking of in the Gospel. This is the freedom Jesus desires for us as well.

Today I will ask Jesus to help me to see some way in which I could live and love more freely.

Readings: Daniel 3:14–20, 91–92, 95; Daniel 3:52–56; John 8:31–42

Trust

"I do know him and I keep his word."
—John 8:55

There is a place in my heart where I know with peaceful clarity who I am and what I am about. Through storms of doubt and fear, through the jaded voices of those who do not welcome the ways of God, I can pass unshaken.

Like Jesus, I need only cling to the Word planted in me. I need only trust the God whose love I know, the God who knows me well, the God whose promise sustains me.

Breathe in and pray: I do know God.
Breathe out and pray: I keep God's word.

Readings: Genesis 17:3–9; Psalm 105:4–9; John 8:51–59

Faithfulness

"Even though you do not believe me,
believe the works...."
—John 10:38

"Don't talk of love—*show me*!" sings Eliza Doolittle in *My Fair Lady*. When Tevye of *Fiddler on the Roof* asks his wife, "Do you love me?" she answers by pointing to her "works"— washing his clothes, cooking his meals, sharing his bed— works of love performed with faithfulness over countless years.

The deeds that I perform prove how genuine are the values that I proclaim. My everyday actions reveal the person I truly am.

Gracious God, let my words and deeds,
my choices and judgments, reflect your image
to others and reveal to them that I am yours.

Readings: Jeremiah 20:10–13;
Psalm 18:2–7; John 10:31–42

Sign of Contradiction

"It is better for you to have one man die for the people than to have the whole nation destroyed."
—John 11:50

Some see Jesus and his works as bringing light,
others, as danger and threat to the status quo,
catalyst of toppling change.

He stands: scapegoat, target, sign of contradiction.

Those who seek him out and cast their lot with him
are powerless to prevent the drama from playing out
in the dark hours to come.

Yet they see—as does he—
that the tomb of Lazarus is empty.
An even greater sign waits: to break open a dawn
   newer than ages and sages
have ever seen before.

**Ask Jesus for the faith to believe that new life waits to
emerge after a time of confusion and contradiction.**

Readings: Ezekiel 37:21–28; Jeremiah 31:10–13; John 11:45–56

Palm Sunday, *April 1*

Love's Invitation

Jesus said, "Truly I tell you, one of you will betray me, one who is eating with me."
—Mark 14:18

Once again, I am astounded by Jesus! Knowing what he did about Judas, Jesus still continued with this Passover celebration, then generously gave us the legacy of his body and blood. I don't believe that I could have continued on, enjoying the celebration and my friends, if I knew of such betrayal.

Each day we, too, have the opportunity to sit at table with Jesus and receive him in nourishment and strength. What is amazing to me is that we are still invited even though we, too, are betrayers. True, it is in smaller ways, and often unintentional, that we fail in our discipleship. Yet the table remains set; the meal is prepared; our host stands ready; and we are always invited. Worthiness is not the issue for God. Love is!

I pray for humility and gratitude as I celebrate the Eucharist today.

Readings: Matthew 21:1–11; Isaiah 50:4–7; Psalm 22:8–9, 17–20, 23–24; Philippians 2:6–11; Mark 14:1—15:47

In Time and Eternity

*Jesus said, "Leave her alone. She bought
[this perfume] so that she might keep it
for the day of my burial."*
—John 12:7

In a sense, God loves us to death! Loves us to the moment of our last letting-go. Our faith in Jesus Christ walks us into the mystery where Jesus experienced the fullness of God, where God wants us to experience the same. In eternity, God continues to love us into perfection, into wholeness. "Purgatory" is divine love, not divine wrath.

So I continue to believe and hope and live and wait until I stand at the threshold. And with God's grace, let go into the arms of that fullness.

Today I will simply hold my hands open, praying to receive the fullness of God...the grace I need most.

Readings: Isaiah 42:1–7; Psalm 27:1–3, 13–14; John 12:1–11

Unconditional Love

Peter said to [Jesus], "...I will lay down my life for you." Jesus answered, "...Before the cock crows, you will have denied me three times."
—John 13:37–38

Peter really does love Jesus. He means well, yet he overestimates himself time and again. Jesus named him "Rock." Was Jesus overestimating Peter? I don't think so. Jesus saw who Peter could and would become...through experience and grace.

Peter's weakness and ours is an opportunity to encounter grace. We are invited to live our weakness, our brokenness, with the blessing of God, who knows who we are and who we can become. As shamed and humiliated as Peter must have been when he heard the cock crow, he had to decide: leave or, as the story goes, swim to the shore when Jesus appeared.

Peter teaches us to trust in God; Jesus teaches us that God's love is unconditional. Peter learned not only his total dependence on God, but that God is totally dependable.

Today I pray to see myself from God's point of view.

Readings: Isaiah 49:1–6;
Psalm 71:1–6, 15, 17;
John 13:21–33, 36–38

Choosing Jesus

*"The one who has dipped his hand into
the bowl with me will betray me."*
—Matthew 26:23

This Gospel story is one of the most painful in all of the Christian Scriptures. In it we see Jesus, hours before his passion and death, freely choosing to rescue us from the tyranny of hatred, duplicity, and all other forms of evil. Here, sharing a last meal with his chosen twelve, he knows the heart of each, including Judas, his betrayer.

Jesus' sadness is palpable to all as he acknowledges that one who has broken bread with him and shared the cup of blessing will send him to his death. As we meditate on this tragic moment do we dare ask, Have I ever betrayed you, Lord? Is sin in any of its myriad forms a part of my life? How committed am I to reject sin with the help of God's grace?

**Lord, help me this Holy Week to see sin in my life
as you see it and make a firm resolve to be
faithful to our commitment to you.**

Readings: Isaiah 50:4–9; Psalm 69:8–10, 21–23, 31, 33–34; Matthew 26:14–25

The Dignity of Service

"So if I, your Lord and Teacher, have washed your feet, you also ought to wash one another's feet."
—John 13:14

At the Passover supper Jesus establishes a new covenant between God and humanity by offering his body that would be broken and his blood that would be poured out for us, his friends. That covenant, which intimately binds us to God and God to us, transcends the chasm between Creator and creature. To illustrate how far God will go to save us, Jesus then carries out the lowliest task in his culture, a task performed by non-Jewish slaves. The Son of God bends down in front of us, cleansing us, preparing us for our new life as the ransomed daughters and sons of God. In that act, he demonstrates the dignity of the life of service to which we are called.

May our love of God be expressed in service to our sisters and brothers, loving God "with the strength of our arms and the sweat of our brow" (Saint Vincent de Paul).

Readings: Exodus 12:1–8, 11–14; Psalm 116:12–13, 15–18; 1 Corinthians 11:23–26; John 13:1–15

At the Cross Her Station Keeping...

*Standing near the cross of Jesus
[was] his mother....*
—John 19:25

In the end there is only the Son and his mother. They inhabit a country all their own, an island of peace amidst a sea of confusion and violence. Death is happening in this moment, but Life will mysteriously, and forever, triumph.

Mothers and sons often have complicated relationships. Sons mature, leave home, and embark on lives far from the safety and security their mother's love once ensured. The love of Jesus and Mary survives distance and renown. It is a love of utter simplicity, grounded in the "yes" each has spoken to their Abba. They have no need of words to understand each other, but words are necessary for the sake of those who will claim discipleship down through the generations. "Behold your mother," Jesus says, and gives Mary to John, and us, to be our mother, guide, support.

**Jesus, let me be with Mary and learn from her
what it means to be faithful.**

Readings: Isaiah 52:13—53:12;
Psalm 31:2, 6, 12–13, 15–16, 17, 25;
Hebrews 4:14–16, 5:7–9; John 18:1–19, 42

Of Stones and Love

*"Who will roll away the stone for us from
the entrance of the tomb?"*
—Mark 16:3

A question only, not a deterrent, asked by the women in
the predawn darkness of that first day. Urged on by their
profound love of the crucified one, they let the question
hover around the edge of their determination to perform
the final act of reverence for the body of the Lord. Love
kept them going despite the seemingly insurmountable
obstacle they knew lay in their way.

The question shapes the context of our faith life as
well. We can name the stones that so often block the
entrance of our heart and prevent us from accepting the
possibility of resurrection. But when our desire for God is
strong enough, deep enough, we too find that the stone
has already been moved away.

What stones keep *me* from encountering the living Lord Jesus?

Readings: Genesis 1:1—2:2;
Genesis 22:1–18; Exodus 14:15—15:1;
Isaiah 54:5–14; Isaiah 55:1–11;
Baruch 3:9–15, 32—4:4;
Ezekiel 36:16–28; Romans 6:3–11;
Psalm 118:1–2, 16–17, 22–23;
Mark 16:1–8

Easter Sunday, *April 8*

In the Light of a New Day

The stone had been removed from the tomb.
—John 20:1

Sometimes we choose to stay in our self-made tombs. We hold on to old hurts, to regrets, to "if onlys." We sometimes let ourselves be buried in the pain of the past and have come to define ourselves by our injuries. Easter is the moment to recognize that the stone has been rolled back and we have an opportunity to leave our tombs of grudges held and wrongs unforgiven. How free it feels to walk in the light of a new day with the risen Lord! How wonderful to breathe deeply of new possibilities given to us! Celebrate today as an opportunity to leave behind any bitterness and resentment that bind us. Take some concrete step today to begin to forgive and become free from all that enslaves us. God has rolled the stone away; we must exit the tomb.

This is the day that the Lord has made, let us rejoice and be glad! Alleluia, Alleluia, Alleluia! (Psalm 118:24)

Readings: Acts 10:34, 37–43; Psalm 118:1–2, 16–17, 22–23; Colossians 3:1–4; Mark 16:1–8

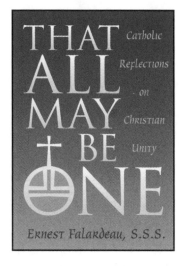

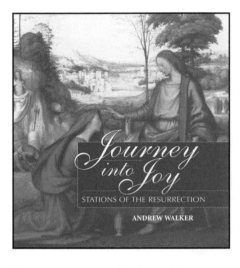

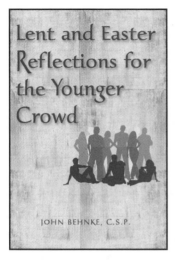

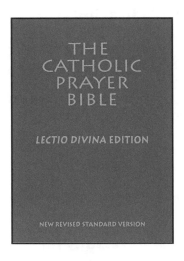
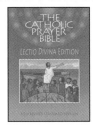

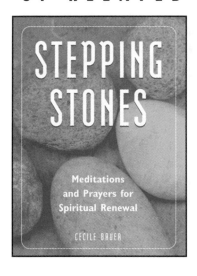

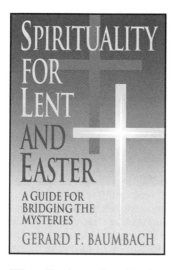

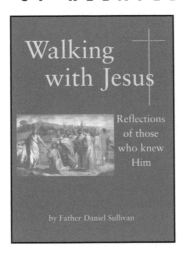

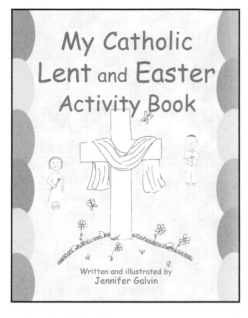

Makes a Great Gift!

Living the Days of Lent 2013

Paulist's best-selling series of daily Lenten devotions uses scripture, prose reflections, and original prayers and poems to center readers' minds and souls and gently bring them to readiness for Easter. With these daily meditations, readers learn to open themselves to the risks and rewards of living a fuller life, of finding compassion from themselves and others, and of resting more deeply in God's loving care.

Living the Days of Lent 2013—

- runs daily from Ash Wednesday through Easter Sunday.
- ends each day's selection with the daily lectionary citations.
- includes pointed challenges for one's thoughts and actions.
- comes in a tear-out, page-a-day format for handy use.

-------------------------------- *Reserve Your Copy Today!* --------------------------------

Please send me _____ copy(ies) of: **Living the Days of Lent 2013**
#978-0-8091-4746-5 @ $4.95 ea.

Please include applicable sales tax, and postage and handling ($3.50 for first $20 plus 50¢ for each additional $10 ordered)—check or money order only payable to **Paulist Press.**

Enclosed is my check or money order in the amount of $ _____

Name _____

Position _____

Institution _____

Street _____

City/State/Zip _____

Phone # _____

For more information or to receive a free catalog of our publications, contact us at:

 Paulist Press™ 997 Macarthur Blvd., Mahwah, N.J. 07430 • 1-800-218-1903
FAX 1-800-836-3161 • E-MAIL: info@paulistpress.com • www.paulistpress.com
Prices subject to change without notice.